BE YOUR OWN COME UP

Beyond Sex, Scams, and Survival

By Andrea C. Toussaint

Leslie,
Thanks so much for always being an inspiration. You're made it possible for so many of us to dream bold dreams. I appreciate the support.
With love,
Andrea

You have to be someone.

~Bob Marley

FOREWORD

A note from Gloria Carter...

I met Andrea sixteen years ago; at the time she was an educator at Boys & Girls High School. From the moment I met her, I knew that there was something very special about her. As I watched her from the distance, I noticed that the young people were gravitating towards her like flies to honey. I later found out that her passion was uplifting young people, motivating them to be all they can be, not just by talking to them but also being there with them every step that they took.

She put these young people before herself, fighting against overwhelming odds and she still forged forward. She has now become a phenomenal woman who deserves to be recognized for her contribution to the world of young people. Her book Be Your Own Come Up speaks loud and clear to who she truly is...AMAZING!!!

Congratulations,
Gloria Carter
CEO of the Shawn Carter Foundation

A note from Carolyn Archer...

Kudos to Andrea!!!

With raw and rare sensitivity shown in this current age, Andrea presents a focused and novel approach to age-old human flaws: low self-esteem and lack of self-confidence. In Be Your Own Come Up Andrea speaks very personally and candidly to her generation and is unapologetically transparent in sharing herself, her life experiences, and her spirituality in this project.

Be Your Own Come Up is a keeper! It is a tool to inspire, challenge, and teach the reader that you are unique, fearfully and wonderfully made and that there is a promise on your life to live in abundance—in your oneness and your individuality. Most importantly, she conveys that there really is "GOOD" in good-bye.

I am very proud to be part of the village that has provided the inspiration, the motivation, and the boldness shown by this young woman in writing this book. Andrea, thank you for stepping up and stepping out. Keep walking in faith, Sunshine!

Blessings always,
Carolyn Archer

For my parents because you have *always* believed in me!

I'm far from finished love bugs …

and you better be here for the ride!

I love you Fran and Big Bear.

Always … Drea

Table of Contents

Something Like An Intro: Roses Do Grow through Concrete

In May of 1996, my father called my sisters and I to the kitchen and handed us a magazine. On the cover was a beautiful brown girl in her high school graduation regalia. Her smile reinforced the importance of that moment. However, as my eyes shifted left, the title of the article countered the beautiful image. The young woman was featured on the magazine not to recount her high school success and college matriculation but to share her story of how love and naiveté left her hostage to a man and a situation that spiraled out of control. Beyond the beauty of the picture was an ambitious college student who fell prey to the trappings of scamming, survival, and sex. Before she knew it, she was slapped with a twenty-four-and-a-half year prison sentence.

As we neared the end of our forced read aloud, I found myself in a conundrum. There was beauty to the lure of the game—the idea of living fast and acquiring material wealth; however, that idea was quickly overshadowed by the thought of the consequences. Riddled with fear, it was clear that I had, at 15 years old, made a conscious decision to get my entire life together. This young woman's story helped to redirect my semi-damaged perspective. I had recently been suspended from one school and reluctantly accepted by my neighborhood zone school. My days of cutting class, smoking weed, and hanging out had come to a close. And, with the end of sophomore year approaching, I knew I had much to recover to ensure I positioned myself for success.

Although I had the support of my parents and family, the work was mine alone to do. As I struggled to redefine myself, I latched on to the words of my elders and became a more avid reader. At the time, the urban novel had become a huge phenomenon and Tyree's *Fly Girl*, Shange's *For Colored Girls*, Wood's *True to the Game*, sapphire's *Push*, and Souljah's *No Disrespect* and *Coldest Winter Ever* provided the impetus to further aid in my coming of age. By the time I was 17 one thing was clear: I would be my own come up and, it is from that place I write these pages.

After 16 years as an educator in New York City, I have come to witness a false dichotomy in the way we approach raising our girls. I have encountered some of the most incredible young people—especially my girls. As I developed relationships with them, however, I noticed an emptiness that resided beyond the surface. Behind the makeup, outfits, status in clubs/organizations, participation in athletics, and fast talk was a void that required much to assuage. Oftentimes, many of these beautifully packaged—but secretly damaged—young women neglected their pain and were left to make decisions that ultimately altered the course of their lives.

With that understanding and perspective, I write this book for all young women who are trying to see beyond the confines of current circumstances—the roses who will defy the odds and burst through the concrete manifesting their beauty and splendor. As you exist in this space you will see your life shift. Will it always be unicorns and rainbows? Absolutely not! However, there is comfort in knowing you have made your own decisions. What life has taught me is that when we embrace *who* we are, *whose* we are, and *what* we have been charged to do, we will begin to see the collateral beauty in all things.

Now, the title of this book is intentional and I'm sure there are some who have shied away from picking it up because it hit a nerve. Others may see it as an assault on their being. I cannot force you to see the world through my lens, but I know as you engage in this reading, either publicly—on the train to work or school—or privately—on your Kindle cause you are cussing me in your head—I'm sure you would agree with much of what is presented. We have to teach our girls to do better so they become better. There is no other way for us to begin to re-imagine the world in which our children must live.

However, *Be Your Own Come Up: Beyond Sex, Scams and Survival* has two purposes. I want every little girl to be confident in her being. I want her to embrace her light and learn to navigate the difficult and thorny patches that life will throw her way, secure in knowing her tomorrows can and will be better.

I need our girls to understand that if they are patient with themselves and the process they will reap the rewards this life has prepared for them. While they wait, however, they have to demonstrate faith and not rush because they can mess up their entire lives by moving in haste, hanging out with people who have no goals or ambition, and engaging in activities that break them down instead of building them up.

Secondly, if more of our girls come into adulthood with a sound sense of self, they will refuse to settle. And when they don't settle, our young men will have to step up too—making this change two-fold. If we encourage our girls to be better, our young men will have to strive to become their best selves because our girls will have requirements and standards for our young men to meet. In the end, our girls and boys will want better for each other and the paradigm will begin to shift. It's simple math ... and I honestly think it can balance the equation.

We won't be raising a generation of young people who are book smart but short on common sense. There will be no room for imposter syndrome to set in and destroy their beings. Will one book serve as a panacea? No, but it is the start—the start of important conversations, the start of shifts in thinking, and the start of acting in ways that will move our children into greater spaces. When we are able to do this, sex and using one's body to come up will not be an option. No longer will running scams for material items and the quick come up be an option. Going into survival mode when things get a little difficult will not be an option either, because our children will know who they are and they will not be willing to compromise their integrity for instant gratification.

Although I will not delve deeply into religion and spirituality in this book, it will be the place from where the book opens. Being spiritually grounded has moved my life into places I didn't expect to access. I must attest to how wonderful God has been in my life. God saved me. He redirected my steps on many occasions and helped me to avoid situations, people, and circumstances that could have derailed my purpose. I wasn't the biggest fan of Sunday morning church service with my mom and all the bows and lace. But at 38, I proudly acknowledge and thank both my parents for centering my life in Christ. I am still being shaped by God's word, God's will, and God's ways, but I have come much farther with Him than I would have on my own. His guidance led me to the feet of elders and wise friends who have touched my life in ways I did not know possible.

The chapters in this book build on one another, but if one of the chapter titles speak to you, feel free to start there. There's no perfect plan or pace—it's just a belief in self that will guide you to trust your inner self and come to the realization that you can fulfill your purpose. Chapter 1 talks about the promise that was put on your life before you even came into being. In Chapter 2, I discuss how embracing that promise will lead you to define yourself in ways that will allow you to always choose you first. Chapter 3 builds on the first two chapters, reminding readers that if you choose you and keep your promise central, you will always see the blessing of opportunity in all circumstances—whether it is negative or positive. Chapter 4 presents the importance of embracing your light while making a conscious decision, as outlined in Chapter 5 to do it for the 'Gram, or not. In Chapter 6, I present the story of a young entrepreneur—Ming; who chose to hustle forward and is experiencing great success. Chapter 7 is by far my favorite because you have the space to personalize this book and take from the other chapters to begin the work of being your own come up. In Chapter 8, I offer a charge to you—to reset and restart as you become your own come up!

I hope you enjoy this book as much as I have enjoyed writing it. It captures the light that many of my former students attribute to parts of their growth, healing, and success. With all the peace, joy, and humility I possess, I pray that you, too, are able to find small gems that will aid you in your journey to being your own come up! And so it begins...

Remember...

When we embrace *who* we are,

whose we are, and *what* we have

been charged to do, we will begin

to see the collateral beauty in all

things.

Chapter I

There Is a Promise

Promises are difficult to hold on to because they are often empty. People make promises all the time, but the fulfillment of them is optional, making it hard to trust the word of others. My parents always told me that promises were made to be broken and in the human form they were correct. My mom promised to take me to June Balloon as a kid and I'm still waiting to go (those of you born after 1995 probably know nothing about). It doesn't mean that she was a bad parent because she was and is more than amazing. It was just that in her day-to-day obligations, getting to the Brooklyn Museum on that specific day never occurred. I also think it was her way of getting us to shape up, because we definitely looked forward to going and we knew all chores had to be completed and our behavior had to be up to par. To this day, we still laugh about it.

Nevertheless, if we take a look at the definition of the word promise, there are two words often included—declaration and assurance. To appreciate the idea of a promise, we have to unpack the notion that there is a thing that has been declared and there is some sort of assurance the thing will materialize. When people are expected to do something and it doesn't come to pass, what surfaces is great disappointment and little assurance.

The reality is that without a contract or legal document, promises can be broken. Nonetheless, there is one who can make a declaration over our lives who will assure the dreams and desires of our hearts come to pass. We must understand that a declaration and assurance of greatness was placed on our lives before we were born—it is the most important promise we could have been given. Parents are responsible for one part of the promise because they are supposed to ensure we are cared for and our needs are met. However, total fulfillment of the promise over our lives is outside of their earthly work and abilities.

Because there is a promise on our lives, it is important for me to acknowledge the presence of a higher force: God. God, I believe, has bestowed upon me a promise for my life. Although I know there is a promise, I am fallible in that I can't understand why it takes so long for certain things to unfold. Over time I came to understand that the promise on my life would not materialize on my time, which is a difficult idea to comprehend because it requires waiting. There were days when waiting in faith and with patience was an arduous task.

Although frustration and fear, the products of the wait, were real, I learned that sometimes it isn't about the answer to the prayer. I found much more value in what I learned while I was waiting for the answer. Despite the length of the wait or the magnitude of my frustrations, I realized the answer would always come because God promised it. We just have to be keen listeners—and that listening includes hearing those we don't want to hear, because there is value in their word when it is properly deciphered and deconstructed.

When we were born, though, God put a promise in our hearts. Not one of us was overlooked. He gave each of us His best and that is the most important takeaway from this chapter. If we know that we have His blessing, more than half of the battle is won. Although every circumstance we face will be viewed through a different lens, what remains is the promise for greatness in our lives. The promise doesn't mean we will get everything right, or that we will get everything we want. It simply means that we are protected and we will always be able to recover and rebound. That promise is the foundation of any come up!

The promise guarantees we have the necessary resources at our disposal, but we also have to be willing to do the work. Our human resources should be counted in family, mentors, and friends because this is our most important social capital. For me, family is everything—they are my greatest blessing. My people are not perfect, but they have been more than enough. We may fight and argue, but our love is much thicker. We find time for each other and we know we can depend on our bond to carry us through. There is no decision, no problem, no issue I fear bringing to them because they are the ones who help me to sift through feelings of insecurity, shame, or guilt. The great thing about family is that they, too, understand the promise on our lives. What we will find is that in both their praise and their reproach they also redirect our focus to the promise on our lives. Count your blessings in them—in all of their perfectly imperfect ways.

For some, however, the ways in which family have failed us makes it difficult to trust their guidance. Nevertheless, we have to pay attention to the lessons despite the pain. Harping on the pain can force us into survival mode or coerce us to use scamming and sexing to get beyond the hurt. In the absence of a sound familial core, we should seek out mentorship from adults who have shown particular interest in our wellbeing. The extended family-like relationships developed through mentoring can and will impact our lives in profound ways.

My mentors have been a blessing from God. I've managed to surround myself with people who have been extremely instrumental in my come up. My mentors have provided a balance in criticism and care that allow me to dream beyond and see beyond the self-imposed and socially bestowed confines. They have helped me to dream boldly and dare greatly, despite the fear of failure. Through mentorship we build character and we learn to grow because in these relationships there is an expectation for us to maximize our potential. Serving as an extension of us, our mentors allow us to see ourselves in different lights. While providing the scaffolds and encouragement to stretch us and move us out of our comfort zone, their support helps us refine our belief in ourselves while assisting in the actualization of the promise on our lives.

In addition to mentors, the people we identify as friends are also significant. My circle of friends has shifted throughout my life, but there are five women whose friendships have been consistent. Genesa, Tamika, Margaret, Isha and Delissa are more than friends. Over the years, they have become my sisters. They have seen me at my best and my worst, yet they love me anyway. With all of my mixed moods and attitudes, their friendship and sisterhood have been consistent. Although there is an energy I am able to exchange with these women that is nothing short of magic, not all of our friendships will be able to withstand life's circumstances.

We must know that friends can be fickle and our circle of friends will forever change—some will be there for the long haul and others will fall out of sync at their appointed times. I often find myself giving people positions in my life they do not deserve. My ex used to call it my "tear for the world". Because he knew my heart, he was able to see the warning signs flashing over the heads of friends long before I did. While we were together, there were several people I called friend, but he always called the friendship's end way before I saw it.

To this day, he is one of my most trusted advisors who never hesitates to weigh in on any aspect of my life, and he has proven to be one of the best friends I could have ever been blessed to have. At the end of friendships I treasured, he would reframe the loss and simply remind me of the blessing associated with tightening up my circle. He also told me that the shifts and departures were God's way of making room for those who truly deserved to be in my space. Although this was difficult for me to accept, with each goodbye I found myself moving one step closer to the promise on my life being realized.

When friendships end, we have to focus on what replaces those who depart from our lives—therein lies the blessing. Think about the ways we have been able to grow when we let go of people who are not a part of the fulfillment of our promise. For example, the recent loss of one friend has afforded me the opportunity to gain sisterhood and accountability partners in four other women: Natascha, Russelle, Quinn, and Krystal. Instead of being bitter about the end of one friendship, I placed more value on the existing ones and thanked God for blessing me with new lifelines. In these new bonds, I've encountered women who would help me to grow in the next chapter of my life.

Natascha and I were frenemies for years, without reason. However, when we began working at a new school together we managed to sift through the mess and create a beautiful and mutually supportive friendship. Russelle has been a sounding board as I navigate the problems I create for myself—yep, at 38 it still happens because perfection does not exist; no one is perfect. In our initial conversation, Quinn shared with me a line from a documentary she had recently watched that shapes my approach to fights. Loosely quoted she said, "Pick your enemies carefully. How they fight is who you will become." And Krystal has been my accountability partner and sister as we navigate our doctoral studies at Columbia—it was she who told me, "You can't be a demon to yourself and an angel to others." The goal here is to surround ourselves with people who will help us to move into different places and tap into different spaces as we elevate and evolve.

And, that's the other thing when it comes to those we call friends. Always remember, just because we are a friend to someone, it doesn't mean they are a friend to us. All relationships are not evenly yoked. When they are not, they are destined to end. We have to learn to embrace the absence if we want to experience the fulfillment of the promise. The loss will be painful but the lesson will be priceless. Remember, because humans are fallible, we have to be selective about the depth of our friendships because all things have an expiration date.

The upside, however, is that in addition to family, mentors, and friends, our intellectual resources are equally important. You're brilliant! I hope I'm not the first person to tell you this and if I am, at least now you know. When we accept our brilliance we come to believe a very simple idea: Invest in your brain, not your bag. This whole new age concept of the bag is very deceiving. Literally and physically, bags are material items designed to store and carry stuff. Bags, like many other treasured material items, lose their value. However, when we invest in our brains, we are nurturing something that can produce, manifest, and grow. When we invest in our brains, the bag will come. Building our mental muscle provides security that a scam, sex, or survival could ever assure. As we build our intellectual resources, we will learn to tap into talents, possibilities, and ideas we probably never knew existed.

There's one final, but important, note about promises: we must always consider the promises we make to ourselves. As much as possible, with other people breaking their promises, we have to commit to fulfilling the promises we make to ourselves. If we're doing what feels good in our hearts and souls, we are moving toward fulfilling the promise on our lives. If we allow our insecurities to dominate our being we will doubt our abilities, disregard our promise, and delay our blessings.

For every problem, every heartache, every situation ... there is a promise, and that promise is always embedded in love! I remember sitting, crying, outside of Antioch Baptist Church with one of my mentors for about an hour because I felt like life was handing me a raw deal. As she allowed me to cry, she used that moment to remind me of the promise on my life. She told me that my ability to believe I was not forgotten and I was not here to suffer and live in lack should always serve as the reminder that I was loved by the most important person in this world—God. She encouraged me to never lose sight of what God had ordained for my life—the declaration and assurance that the promise would be fulfilled. In her mothering nature, Ms. Archer told me to meditate on Psalms 23, 91, and 121 whenever I felt like giving in to doubt because, in those scriptures, God's promise is reiterated.

We must always remember that we have exactly what we need to fulfill the promise on our lives. It's within. When I take time to be reflective, I remind myself of my purpose and the promise for my life becomes clear. Take a moment and list your strengths ... think about all the things that will make your wildest dream a reality. You are intelligent. You are charismatic. You are personable. You are a good listener. You are articulate. You are hardworking. You are patient. You are dedicated. You are creative. You are beautiful. You are humble. You are human. Tap into those characteristics because they will bring long-term success, not fleeting things.

As Anais Nin said, "Life expands and contracts in proportion to our courage." That courage is embedded in the promise on our lives, should we choose to embrace it. When we embrace our promise and chart our own course, the journey will be rewarding. Yes, we will experience loss, but it is a part of managing our own satisfaction. We have to come to a place where we can train our mind to see the good in everything and adopt the attitude, "I can because I believe I can." In so doing, we live, we learn, and we level up!

Remember...

When you were born, God put a

promise in your heart. It is a

promise that can be fulfilled!

Chapter II

Define You, Choose You!

It's human nature to prioritize everything and everyone before us. But in claiming the promise on our lives, we must remember to put ourselves first. When we consider ourselves in all things we become a priority—we have to be our most important investment. How we define ourselves determines what we accept, what we value, and how much we are willing to invest in us. If we focus solely on the things we find wrong with us, we will never find the beauty of our spirit. We will never tap into the essence of our lives and being. We will never be able to accentuate the positive in us. Affirming soul deposits are vital.

Only when we are able to define who we are and what we want to do for ourselves will we be putting ourselves first. "I matter." We have to get in the habit of saying to ourselves every morning, "I matter and I'm worth it!" because we do matter and our lives have worth, purpose, and meaning. When we embrace this idea, we will see things shift because light attracts light. It doesn't matter what the circumstances are, once we project positivity we come to expect it. More importantly, we begin to choose ourselves first, ultimately allowing ourselves to define who we are on our own terms. We cannot be our own come up if external factors define *the who* we are in the moment and *the who* we are to become in the future.

We have to tell ourselves that we are going to define who we are without interference. We have to believe that who we are is based on what and who we allow in our space. When we define ourselves, we are unapologetically ourselves and people must come to accept us as we are. We can never allow ourselves to feel compelled to conform to the standards of others. I'm not saying we have to refrain from liking or accepting others. We will regularly encounter people we believe have something we may want to assimilate into our character and that is totally fine. In defining ourselves, we have to look at the world and choose what is right and what is wrong as it pertains to our well being.

When defining ourselves, it is important for the definition to be grounded in the promise we already know is on our lives. When the promise is central, we will always look at the positive contributions we make. In so doing, we inevitably come to realize the essence of who we are. The definition is important because the words we speak over our lives have the power to manifest in ways that will have a profound impact on our come up.

We must understand the ways in which we define ourselves—what we expect, what we accept, what we do, who we do it with, and where we do it will play into the definition. And, we have to make sure the definition is one we can live with. It will be a definition that shows the world how we feel about ourselves. We do not have to tell others the definition because the way we act and the way we carry ourselves will be a testament. When we respect ourselves, the definition of our self leads with an air of worth. Remember, there is power in the definition, so we must use that power wisely.

Now, being able to create this definition does not mean dark days and tough times will not be ours. Because we accept and acknowledge the promise that is on our lives and we have elected to define who we are on our own terms, we will come to navigate difficulties with confidence. We will understand that tough times will not mark our entire lives, but these times will be an important part of our journeys. In darkness is the opportunity for growth and the ability to emerge stronger. During these seasons, it is important to engage in periods of reflection and separation.

Reflection affords the opportunity for purposeful consideration of all things. Much is to be learned when time is invested in considering the why and the how of our actions or inaction. Some of the most valuable lessons are learned when time is allotted to sitting alone and engaging in thought-provoking consideration about who we are, where we are, and how we get to where we want to be. Reflection helps deepen our understanding of what we know while allowing us to identify what we do not know (our gaps in knowledge). When things are difficult, reflection is critical because we begin to consider the ways in which we have strayed from the direction we created for ourselves. What often happens after reflection is that we come to a place where separation becomes inevitable.

Although separation can be viewed as a negative and elitist idea, it is actually one of the only things that allows us to move from one place in our lives to the next. If we never separate from people, refrain from certain behaviors, or stop going to certain places, we will stifle our ability to grow. This idea is reminiscent of the story of lobsters and how they grow—I know, I never considered how lobsters grow until a professor shared Rabbi Dr. Abraham Twerski's YouTube video with our class. In the video, Dr. Twerski describes lobsters as soft and mushy animals that live in a rigid shell that does not expand. However, as the lobster begins to grow the shell becomes confining and impedes the ability to expand. Feeling under pressure and uncomfortable, the lobster goes under a rock to protect itself, casts off the old shell, and produces a new one. The lobster continues to go through this process throughout its lifetime Like the lobster, this process is applicable to us.

In order to elevate, we have to separate from certain people and remove ourselves from certain situations. I'm not saying we are better than another person or that we have to cut ties with everyone who is not moving in our direction, but we do have to be cognizant of the roles we allow people to assume in our lives. It's okay to have those who constructively influence our lives, those who speak abundance and positivity over us. Others, however, have to be relegated to a certain space so they do not strip us of our energy or cause us to revert to old ways of thinking, old ways of knowing, and old ways of being.

When we engage in these two critical activities— purposeful reflection and purposeful separation—we choose us first, without reservation. "Choosing me" means we are putting ourselves first, and that is probably the most powerful thing we can do. My cousin Karen would always say lead with the hashtag, "#ichooseme". No one else will prioritize us the way we deserve to be prioritized. We always want to make sure we put ourselves in a position to be the priority and not the option.

Optional things get done whenever we find time to get them done. Priorities take precedent!

In this case, and this is a very rare instance, being number one matters. It matters because it means that we matter enough to put ourselves in a position to ensure that we are taken care of. It's difficult to prioritize ourselves because sometimes we get so caught up in doing for others and being all things to everyone else that we forget we matter. However, when we define ourselves, we always choose us FIRST.

Remember...

You have to tell yourself that you are going to define who you are on your own terms. When you define yourself, you say to yourself that you are unapologetically you and people must come to accept you as you are.

Chapter III

As Bad as It Is,

Is as Bad as It's Not

56

When we recognize the promise on our lives, we begin to realize we can conquer almost anything that arises. Even though there is a promise and we are working to fulfill that promise, it does not mean obstacles will not surface. In the midst of a conversation with one of my mentors, Gloria Carter, she said, "As bad as it is, is as bad as it's not." I'm sure I was talking about a relationship gone awry and the ways in which my life was slowly coming to an end (LOL). But, in her calm, gentle, and nurturing way, those were the words she uttered and they have had a lasting effect on how I approach difficult situations.

Oftentimes the tape that plays in our heads says our situation is horrible and we are unable to see how things could ever get better. However, the reality is our situation could be worse—think about it. We could be lacking in more ways than we feel we are at that moment. But, if we remember the promise on our lives and we define the way we want to live on our terms, then as bad as it is, is really as bad as it is not! Besides, if we focus on how bad, how messy, and how awful it is, we will give up. We can't come up if we give up.

At this very moment, I have been struggling with ensuring I work toward fulfilling my own goals while finding ways to support those I encounter. I come from a place where I genuinely want to see everyone around me winning. However, what I have found is that the way I pour into people and try to match their energy is not always reciprocated. This stings. I mean, I have had days when I had to force the tears to stop because I had to face the world, and there are nights when the hours aren't long enough to get all the tears out.

As tough as it may be, I have to push myself to see beyond the negative and not feed into idle talk. I have to admit this is something that, at times, I have allowed to bother me. Despite how awful and difficult those moments are, I have learned to remind myself that it's just a moment and I will eventually step out of the darkness because things could be worse. Work, relationships, family, and even writing this book have, at times, tested my faith and my ability in profound ways. Yet, the promise on my life reminds me that there are many more beautiful moments ahead.

Thus, how we think about who we are has an immense part to play in our rise. It's not about what manifests materially, but the ways in which we sow into who we are and the ways we find the strength to withstand moments where we experience a lack. When we understand that things can be worse, we develop more appreciation for the now. It's like the old question: *is the glass half full or half empty?* Perspective, in this case, becomes vital because we grow to understand that where we are and what we have is actually more than enough. I think our ability to accept this idea is the real game changer.

With this realization, we begin to approach life differently. We come to see the beauty of life in moments of scarcity and moments of abundance because we realize we have dominion over our world. I think we might appreciate the moments of abundance even more and move through life with a spirit of gratitude when we learn to use our valley moments to weather life's ups and downs. When work becomes too much or school is stressing us out, remember it could be worse. When the relationship is not right and we feel like life is crumbling, remember it is not as bad as it seems. All situations shift—we just have to demonstrate a level of patience with ourselves and understand that within life's cycles, we must embrace periods of stagnation to appreciate periods of growth.

I don't know if Ms. Carter, my mentor, recognized the power she released in my life that day. For her, it was probably just another opportunity to sow into a young woman a lesson she had learned at some point in her life. However, I grew leaps and bounds when I came to understand and accept those eleven simple words. When faced with difficulty and adversity, I see her smile and I find myself repeating the phrase until clarity comes and pain disappears—for me, in the repetition, I experience a peace that creates serenity and it calms my soul. When we come to truly embrace this principle—as bad as it is, is as bad as it's not—we won't resort to sex, scams, or survival to come up because we know things will get better and we welcome the fact that they are not worse.

The big idea is simple: We have to remember in our valley moments that perspective is everything. If we embrace a deficit model, we will always see the lack. We will search for things to fill the void and when we focus on how bad a thing is, anything can fill the gap—and that's the trap. This is when we rely on and use what we have to get what we think we want. A little sex can get us a couple of dollars. A quick scam and the materialistic things we think give us status and position are ours. In dire circumstances, we shift gears to survival mode where anything goes. However, none of these are options on the way to the come up!

We have to get our swag back, put some pep in our step, and repeat, "as bad as it is, is as bad as it's not." We have to say it until we feel our spirit settling. *Thanks so much Mama G,* because those eleven words will save lives and move individuals to choose differently. I'm pretty sure after reading this there will be a lot of folks sending love and thanks your way.

So, on the road to becoming your own come up, know that there will be moments when you stumble, and those blunders and mishaps can seem earth shattering. However, when we reflect on the essence of what Ms. Carter shared, it may seem bad at the moment but know that it is not. At my age, I still find it difficult to understand why (and how) things shift so quickly from positive to negative, but I've also found the key to understanding lies in perspective. Often what appears to be a negative situation is actually a necessary situation, because out of every disaster is a new beginning.

In the negative, character is developed. Difficult circumstances test our mettle and require grit and resilience to persever. We can't be afraid to use the difficult times to construct a new narrative of self that will help us manifest the fullness of our potential. In moments of difficulty, it is natural to succumb to emotions of fear and search for a quick fix. We must know, however, in these moments that we are receiving

necessary preparation to weather all things because as bad as it

is, baby, is as bad as it's not!

Remember...

You can't come up if you're

going to give up. When you

understand that things can be

worse, you develop more

appreciation for the now.

Chapter IV

Don't Dim Your Light

Don't forget—sometimes our greatest supporters are our biggest naysayers—especially when we are on our journey to better ourselves. They are usually tucked in with the crowd, dressed in a smile with cheers and applause as their accessories. Do not be deceived. Just because they smile with us does not mean they have our best intentions at heart. I'm not saying we should be skeptical of everyone in our circle, but we should be mindful and observant. We can't go into a state of paranoia either, but we must not be naïve. Everyone has an angle. Therefore, we should never, and I mean never, let folks know everything we're thinking or what moves we're planning to make because some, in the shallows of their personal spaces like some will pray on our downfall.

I remember being told by someone I considered a friend that I was "wack". The circumstances around the statement aren't important. What's important is someone I loved uttered the words. After sifting through my personal pain, I realized the venom from their lips was more a reflection of who they were than who I was. As quickly as I heard the words, I dismissed them as their truth and not my own. Trust the elders when you hear them say, "Hurt people, hurt people," because this is a fact. When faced with these moments, though, we still have to love people anyway. This is especially hard to do when we feel personally attacked. It may take time to heal and we will have to vent, but we must also move through it or let the individual go.

We can't allow the joy jippers to snuff the life out of our day, our dreams, or our moments. To combat those difficult times, we must gird ourselves with words of affirmation and encouragement. We will never escape the clutches of the bitter, but the blessed do not beef with the bitter. And remember, we are blessed because we have chosen to acknowledge the promise on our lives. As difficult as it is, we have to love them so we don't break our own spirits. Besides, if we believe in our abilities and ourselves, we will learn to embrace these folks because we will be in a place where we are aware of the shifts as our circle gets smaller.

If we refrain from dimming our lights, we are moving like we love ourselves, we are speaking like we love ourselves, and most importantly, we are acting like we love ourselves. Self-love attracts the light we want to surround us, especially because it illuminates from within. This is the beginning of embracing and protecting our light. Our light is our magic—it is the thing that makes us unique. Remember, light attracts light in the same way darkness envelopes darkness. We must choose whether we want to emit light or dwell in darkness.

We all have a chance to become the person we long to be. The question is, are we willing to take a chance on us? Are we important enough? Do we matter enough to bet on ourselves? If we allow the outside world to define our image, ability, role, past, present, and future, we will never fulfill the promise God has on our lives and our light will never shine. We will be like a hamster running on a wheel getting absolutely nowhere. Remember, dark and distorted glasses are just as damaging as rose-colored glasses. Both will not permit the light that is ours to shine where it should. And, if we are not careful, we will find ourselves making the wrong choices to get to the right place, but in the end, we'll see the sacrifices and compromises were not worth it.

So, ignore the joy jippers—they are simple-minded naysayers. Because of their negative energy, however, they are the ones who can talk us out of our promise due to the dissatisfaction they are experiencing in their own lives. If you happen to consider a joy jipper a friend, you know you have to get rid of them as soon as possible, because we will not fulfill the promise on our lives if we have folks around serving as anchors. We must let them go. Like my mother always says, "You gotta know when to trim the fat." Once we trim the fat, we have to start encouraging ourselves. We have to breathe life into our dreams and our promises. We would not have dreams and promises if they were not going to materialize.

While the outside world can break and fracture our light, they are not the only ones who can. We can, too. We are our toughest critics, and are often very hard on ourselves. However, we cannot be light and have our light shine if we do not learn to nurture it. For me, it is just a force of habit to ensure everyone around me is in a position to succeed. It doesn't matter how big or small the deed, if I can do it, it will be done and I don't expect reciprocation. I have never expected others to sow into me as I have done for them. Over time, I've just learned to move accordingly and continue doing the work while simultaneously nurturing my light—but this is hard and I must admit lonely. Sometimes, I lack patience when shaping my light, but it is a balance I am learning to develop and with the support of family, mentors and a few friends, my dreams have become a reality.

We also have to come to know ourselves in terms of our strengths and limitations. If we do not, other people can penetrate a weak exterior and challenge our being. We can't snuff out our light or allow others to do so either. We must learn to protect our light and learn to let it shine despite the shade and the clouds.

Remember...

Your light is your magic—it is

the thing that makes you unique.

Light attracts light in the same

way darkness envelopes

darkness. You must choose

whether you want to emit light

or dwell in darkness.

Chapter V

Do It for the 'Gram ...

Or Not!

Social media has a profound impact on our thoughts and actions. We see the way people live and we try to find ways to match and exceed these lifestyles. When I was younger, my mother used to say, "Don't envy people for what they have because you never know what they did to get it." I have to admit that I am blessed to have learned this at an early age, because I do not envy people for their material possessions. As a teen it was a lot harder for me to understand this concept because I wanted to have the name-brand denim suits and the latest kicks, too. For most young people, this is often a struggle and I don't know if there is anything I can say that would remedy this feeling. However, I hope there is comfort in knowing that if you work hard you can afford all the things you desire in time.

For this generation, though, posts and likes make all the difference and patience is non-existent. However, we cannot be ruled or rushed by the acquisition of things. I now know what my mother meant when she said, "All things in time." When it is to be ours it will be, until then we must make the best of what we have and know that more will come. If we are working on being our own come up, we will never be overlooked because we are focused on the promise, defining and choosing ourselves while embracing our light.

However, if our smile for social media defines us, we will always be empty. No matter how many likes our pictures receive we will always crave more attention. Social media is an addictive drug and it is killing folks—in heart, in mind, and in spirit. If we look to social media for validation and affirmation, know it will be coming from people who are probably more hurt and damaged than we are. The irony is, the unhealthy competition social media creates places us in a race with ourselves because most people on the other side of the post don't care about who we really are.

I want you to consider this: If I told you most people were living their lives through filters, would you believe me? Now don't get me wrong, I'm up for a good filter because I like my selfies looking right, but my life—how I love, how I live, how I elevate—is a different story. We have to be able to distinguish between what's real and what's fake, and most of what we see on social networks is a farce.

Social media is just a platform where people capture the best parts of their lives, not their full realities. We will never see the scars the makeup covers or the sleepless nights and tears before the turn-up and bottle service. The empty, barren, and broken parts of their lives are never captured and those parts show the sacrifices of self that have to be made to present a false perfection. Always remember, there is a back story, and those are the chapters we don't share publicly. Our authentic self is often hidden.

Some of the saddest people are the ones who have everything on social media. The compromises they have to make along the way drain them of their self-worth, which is only uncovered as they begin to strip back the layers of artifice and sham. We often look at people and measure them in the physical, but more often than not, there is an emptiness that encapsulates their being. Many live to acquire material wealth despite the cost to their souls. Having nice things is great, however, what we do to get them is where the cost often outweighs the benefits.

If we remind ourselves that nothing in life blooms all year round, we'll be more comfortable with who we are and what we have. As a kid, my parents made sure we knew the value of family, community and education. These are the things that are important in my life because my parents stressed their importance instead of material acquisition. Nevertheless, we give material things symbolic meanings when they are simply things— items that do not elevate or reduce our status. However, today's popular culture has a way of placing this idea on its head.

All I'm saying is we don't want to wake up at age 40 and realize we can't do more than put together a dope outfit— which is a talent if you become a professional shopper or a professional buyer with clients. Without clientele though, it's futile. We have to assess where we place value when we consider others and ourselves. If our value is not aligned with our promise and our purpose, we will forever do it for the 'Gram, only to be left empty. I guess we can consider this a moral hazard in that when we think we can get what we want without doing the work, then we will work less or not at all.

Allow me to challenge you. Attempt to post a picture with no makeup, with no filters, and with nothing fancy to help elevate or spark the senses of the masses. Now, right before you press the button to post it, take a moment to evaluate that feeling that makes you hesitate. That feeling right there is what we must overcome. That feeling is what breeds envy, hate, and many more negatives in our day-to-day lives that motivates depression and depletes our self-worth.

Now, upload the picture and become free! No matter how many likes you get, when you see the first like, begin to celebrate the fact that someone is joining in on the celebration of your emancipation. Then, you need to try really, really hard to get your arm behind your neck and pat yourself on the back for honoring your authentic self.

Many people lack self-esteem. They don't feel good about themselves, so they define themselves by the kind of clothes they wear, the kind of car they drive, and the catchy captions they create. They try to pump themselves up to feel better about themselves because they really do not accept who they are—which is rebellion against God and the promise He placed on our lives. If God wanted us to be somebody else, we would not exist. But, He wanted us and He made us to be exactly who we are. To truly understand this, we have to take a break from social media occasionally and focus on us. Do a social media fast, let it go for a while, and learn to do it for you first and the 'Gram second!

Remember...

Social media is just a platform

where people capture the best

parts of their lives, not their full

realities.

Chapter VI

Hustle Backwards?

Never!

There's an anomaly and her name is Ming. Not only is she a dope hairstylist and fashionista, she's also smart, charismatic, and, in my opinion, this young woman is a game changer. I met her a little over a year ago when she styled my hair for my birthday party. I watched as she meticulously navigated my first weave. Her cousin Sinthia warned her that I was nervous and very particular about my hair. Despite the pressure, she helped me settle in and talked me through the steps of my first closure. In the end, after my 22s were swinging, she breathed a sigh of relief as she released her nervous butterflies as well. We laughed and chatted a bit more, but I left knowing there was something special about Ming.

I really wanted to name this chapter, "Be Like Ming" but I realized the purpose of this book is not to merely emulate people or recreate some of the experiences I present here. However, when I think about Ming, I had to tap into that something special. Some people have a light you can't avoid. Ming is one of those people.

In the time that I have come to know Ming, here's what I have learned. She has only been doing hair professionally for a little more than three years. She started in her mom's home and moved to three different salons before recently settling in her own beauty studio in Bedford-Stuyvesant. As we chatted during my second appointment, Ming freely shared her dream of owning her own shop. She talked about the art of hair care in a way most stylists don't. She shared her excitement about attending a cutting class in a few weeks and she was looking into learning how to perfect her lace front wigs as well.

On average she works ten hours a day and spends her down time fulfilling wig orders for her clients. Her passion for hair care at an affordable price is the hallmark of her craft. More importantly, she makes each client feel special and beautiful as she ends most appointments with a photo session. And for clients who hate taking pictures (like me), it is not a chore because she smiles with you and talks you right through it.

But there's more ...Ming's twenty-three. She just turned twenty-three in June. Her age is important because it speaks to her hustle, which is not just for her but for her beautiful daughter, five year old Lani. Yeah...do the math. See, that's why her light illuminates. She lives her life to be better for her daughter who is often in the shop at her mom's leg when she's not in a chair with a book or her iPad, or most impressively navigating one of the model heads as she parts, braids, and experiments with her own styles.

I would stop there, but there's one more quality she possesses that most young people are afraid to exhibit and that's vulnerability. She is not afraid to ask a question. Prior to switching cars, she talked through her options before getting her 2018 Mercedes CLA. When she considered moving to Jersey she shared her thoughts about convenience and being on her own, plus allowing Lani to have more space. She was not embarrassed to share her decision to move back to Brooklyn, where she became a homeowner a few months ago. But, the caveat lies in the humility she possesses. She's definitely in a position to "do it for the 'Gram" and she does. You thought I was gonna say she doesn't, eh? Coupled with her humility is her authenticity. She's twenty-three remember, so she enjoys being a twenty-three year old and all that comes along with it. However, her passion for being the best in her field and providing a better life for her daughter keeps her focused on her goals.

Ultimately, she wants to become the owner of a salon, which I know will be a place for women to unwind and enjoy a glam session. Having already branded her hairline, Ming's Luxe Extensionz™, she has taken the first step in becoming a powerhouse who will dominate her field. She finds a way to bring her friends into the fold by employing them as braiders or color technicians. She taps into others so they can come up with her.

And please do not feel like I'm trying to paint her as perfect, but in the time I have come to know her she has been one to admire. She's regular in the sense that things don't define her. You'll catch her in anything from Fashion Nova to

Balenciaga—however, the acquisition of things does not supersede laying a solid foundation. Yes, she has had setbacks as any young single mom would, but she didn't settle. She didn't use them as a crutch. She came from humble beginnings and she uses that as her anchor. She's Joann's daughter; a young woman from East New York, Brooklyn, who simply never lost sight of the most important rule every parent has shared with their child—dream, always, always, always, dream big! And that's why I share her story, or a small part of her story, with you.

I intentionally named this chapter "Hustle Backwards? Never!" because that's what I came to know about Ming. She hustled forward and used her lemons to make that proverbial lemonade. In life we have two choices, we can master the game or fall back on it ... think about that. Ming is a dope young woman and I am fortunate and blessed to have met her.

I want to let you in on a secret: I stopped writing this book some time ago. I was suffering from serious writer's block. A year ago, however I encountered an energy that tapped into a dream I had shelved. So, in part, you're reading this because of Ming. Passion is contagious … we must surround ourselves with the right energy and when we do, amazing things are bound to happen. As you continue to turn these pages, remember: I want you to find that thing you're passionate about. We have to think about the ways we can constantly reignite the flame so what we desire will manifest. When we set goals, have a purpose, and are true to ourselves in some ways, we will find, like Ming, that despite adversity we can always hustle forward.

Never be afraid to take a leap of faith. Remember, moving backward entails relying on old tricks, negative thoughts, and unhelpful people to move us into great, which is life's biggest oxymoron. In this bleak and doubtful space is futility, and futility breeds stagnation where nothing is allowed to grow. The promise on our lives, however, guarantees we will do great things when we find something we are passionate about and we are willing to do the work. Passion propels purpose and purpose enhances all pursuits. Success does not come overnight, but if we're willing to do the work required, over time our dreams will come to fruition.

The hustle is the work; it is comprised of the grind, the sweat, the time, the network, the tears, and the joy. I don't care what life throws at us, we have to remember *as bad as it is, is as bad as it's not.* Since we know it could be worse, we have to bask in the light that guarantees productivity and progress. With this guarantee, we must avoid hustling backward.

Ming, I want to personally thank you for keeping my hair slayed and for unknowingly encouraging me to finish this project. Check her out y'all. You know I'm here for the shameless plug @hairby.ming. You won't be disappointed.

Remember...

The hustle is the work; it is comprised of the grind, the sweat, the time, the network, the tears, and the joy. You can master the game or fall back on it. Success does not come overnight, but if you're willing to do the work required, over time your dreams will come to fruition.

Chapter VII

A Few Jewels for My

Gems

Dr. Frank Mickens, my former principal and boss, had the most impact on my life when it came to shaping my career as an educator. Despite what his critics would say, Mick, as we fondly referred to him, exemplified the essence of an educator who was dedicated to ensuring children received a quality education while being in a space where they felt safe and supported by adults who truly cared. Mick lived his life for the children he served. Boys and Girls High School was his home and for us, his children, and it was his home as well. He found little ways to encourage us and make us feel like we mattered. He did that by fighting for resources, networking with politicians, implementing dress-for-success programs, and finding the necessary resources to ensure we could compete with the best and the brightest.

But, there was also this little things he did that encouraged me more than the big-ticket items. He had a way with words … and if you knew him, you know why I'm smiling (better yet chuckling) right now. Every year, he would have a new slogan; his pearls of wisdom that served as a reminder of who we were and the work we needed to do to become our best selves. The title of this chapter is borrowed from one of those slogans—to Mick, his children were the "Crown Jewels of Bed-Stuy."

Playing on this idea, I decided to drop a few jewels for you: my gems. It is important for us to gird ourselves with short reminders that allow us to focus, refocus, and/or reset whenever necessary. Also, because I am a teacher at heart, I had to incorporate the space for you to question, respond, explain, reflect, examine, or react to each of the gems. Borrowed from 38 years of living, I hope you find some value in this space. It is yours. We can agree to disagree and I would, of course, love to hear your thoughts as you catch me on the A-train, bump into me while sitting on my parent's stoop, or shoot me an email or DM on IG. Use your lines wisely … space is limited.

You can't always wing it.

You must have goals, accompanied by a purpose. Have a plan that you create for yourself on your own terms. Otherwise, you're walking through life aimless and content with whatever comes your way. You might even allow others to define what you should and shouldn't do. Remember the plan is directly linked to the come up. No one comes up by happenstance. Engage in periodic cycles of reflection and separation—it's the only way to gain clarity.

_____

_____

_____

_____

If it's not working, don't chase it.

Sometimes you will have to abort and reset and that's okay. Not all ideas deserve the same attention and it's more than okay to let go. It will be hard to shake the pain associated with the departure of a thing or a person, but you're going to get tired chasing something that is not for you.

_____

_____

_____

_____

Delayed gratification is okay.

My mother always says, "Nothing happens before its time." If you don't get it right now, that's okay. You have to trust the process. When it is to be, it will come. You can't rush it, nor force it. And, often, delayed blessings are even larger. Embrace the wait! And while you wait, marvel at how much you've grown and all that you've learned. Without the wait, stagnation will eventually take root.

_____

_____

_____

_____

A setback is a setup for something better.

There is nothing wrong with a setback once you frame it the correct way. You have to see the blessing in a setback. There is growth and opportunity in each one. The opportunities will be expansive if you don't sulk and do the "woe is me" thing. I know it sounds simpler than it is, especially in the moment, but you get to look back. You get to reflect—and the beauty in that moment will make it worth it.

_____

_____

_____

_____

Work hard, but don't overwork yourself.

You're no good to yourself or anyone else when you're tired. Don't expend energy on unnecessary activities that don't add to your growth or come up. Remember, you are not damaged or broken in any way. You are perfectly imperfect; simply put, you are perfect just the way you are. Do the work, but balance is everything. *I really need to take my own advice on this one...lol.*

_____

_____

_____

_____

If it makes you feel alive, keep it close.

In a world where there are many things to kill your joy, you have to find things that keep you alive and give you purpose. Nurture the moments and the people who match your energy and bring out your glow. It feels good to have that type of magic around you. But you must also remember: if you feel like it's killing you, let it go.

_____

_____

_____

_____

Make peace with your past.

Your past is important. There are valuable lessons, but you have to make peace with what was and hold fast to what will be. Dwelling in the past causes regret that will kill your spirit and your joy. Again, let it go. Take what you must, but you shouldn't carry what you don't need.

_____

_____

_____

_____

Get to know you, the real you.

Who you are matters. Some days you'll be pleased with the person you are and other days may cause regret—*the story of my life*. But, you have to sift through all of you to get to the real you. There's no other way for you to get to the heart of who you are and who you will become without engaging in this process. The real you may be unrecognizable at times, but when you do become familiar with him or her, you will see the beauty in you. Trust me.

_____

_____

_____

_____

You've got to find something you love.

If you're not passionate about it, it will never make sense. You'll be grinding without purpose. You have to find what you love, because what you love will shape your life. You will look forward to getting up, going out, and doing the work. *Having the opportunity to work with young people has definitely been my calling. No day is perfect, but I have never doubted the fact that God created me to teach and engage with young people. They give me life and keep me young—I'm blessed with the best of both worlds.*

_____

_____

_____

_____

Affirm yourself.

Just do you, boo, and affirm yourself in all things. Affirmation of self allows you to think, believe, and know that all things are possible. You have to move with a spirit of affirmation. Because you have been affirmed by God, affirming and encouraging yourself must become second nature.

_____

_____

_____

_____

Nothing in nature blooms all year round.

If you think you have to be on 365 days a year, you are wrong. This is when you can backslide and start hustling backwards. This is also why it's important to get to know you, because you will learn to be content with who you are, whether you have on baggy sweats or high-end fashion. Keeping up with the Joneses will cause more grief than good!

_____

_____

_____

_____

Don't let your happiness depend on anything outside of yourself.

You must allow yourself to make you happy. Everything resides in you! This is difficult to embrace, but it is necessary. If your happiness comes from things outside of your scope, you will always yearn for a fix. There will always be a need for something to complete you.

_____

_____

_____

_____

You're never boxed in. You always have a choice.

With choice is responsibility, not intention. The road to hell is paved with good intentions. Refrain from being an intentional person. You are always responsible, no matter how you feel. Remember that.

_____

_____

_____

_____

Don't worry. If it's supposed to happen, it will.

Don't expect, release expectations and enjoy the journey. Now, I'm not saying coast through life without a plan. Just know that the journey is always better than the destination. The journey builds character. Have the courage and tenacity to see things through. Once you learn to demonstrate patience, your wildest dreams will become a reality.

_____

_____

_____

_____

Dream. Don't be afraid to dream.

One of your greatest abilities is the ability to dream. With dreams come miracles. Yes, miracles do happen, but don't depend on them to happen. Instead, accompany your dreams with hard work and watch them come to fruition.

_____

_____

_____

_____

Be forgiving.

Foremost, forgive yourself daily—*this is still something I have to work on.* With each day, consider all the ways you have dishonored and disrespected yourself, and be forgiving of you first. If you can forgive yourself, it will be easier to forgive others. You have to be willing to meet the unkind and hurtful deeds of others with forgiveness, too. Don't let yesterday's mishaps steal the joys and blessings of a new day—*don't worry I told you... I'm still working on this one, too.*

_____

_____

_____

_____

The greatest theft of joy is comparing yourself to others.

You can't compare yourself to anyone else because you were born to stand out. You don't want to postpone your joy by trying to measure up to people who really don't matter in relation to your come up. Remember you are unique and the promise on your life will always make you different if you choose to embrace it.

_____

_____

_____

_____

Intuition is not to be ignored.

This is how we fail. This is what leads us into situations and circumstances where life gets out of control. You have to trust your gut! You are always free to choose, but you are not free from the consequences of your choice. In all things, although you will strike out occasionally, try to be on the right side of things. Sometimes you can't even trust what you see ... even salt looks like sugar, Suga.

_____

_____

_____

_____

Your elders...they know what they're talking about.

Your parents and the elders in your life don't always get it right, but there is value in what they bring to the table. Good or bad, learn from the lesson. They have the experience—remember they've been your age, you have not been theirs. Look at their circumstances and, reserving judgment, see the ways they have been shaped by their experiences and pull the lessons from the wisdom they share.

_____

_____

_____

_____

Why buy it when you can build it.

When you invest in you, you tap into your talents and find ways to build the empire you desire. You like dope shirts, design them. Whatever you think of, know that it can become a reality. Remember you are filled with infinite possibilities and enough creativity to make any dream a reality.

_____

_____

_____

_____

Surround yourself with people who see your greatness.

Your circle is important. The people in your circle feed you and you have to make sure they are not making you sip poison. People are very fickle, and some don't want to see you win. I'm not saying cut off the world, but, if they don't see your greatness, don't try to change them. Love them anyway for exactly who they are. In time, hopefully they will do the same thing!

_____

_____

_____

_____

It is never too late to become who you want to be.

Don't give up on you. Bet on yourself—it's the greatest investment you'll ever make. The right people will notice, don't worry. Do not resist change. Change is the only real constant in life.

_____

_____

_____

_____

Wake up every morning with a grateful heart.

Every day is a new day. Be grateful that you are allowed to wake up and live. Take full advantage of the opportunity and know that with each day, there is a new opportunity to fulfill the promise on your life as you move toward being your own come up!

_____

_____

_____

_____

Remember...

It is important to gird yourself

with short reminders that will

allow you to focus, refocus,

and/or reset whenever

necessary!

Chapter VIII

Be Your Own Come Up:

A Fresh Start

So, where do you start? The reset and reboot are difficult but necessary. I don't care what your age is, it is always possible to start anew. It's about being willing to take that first step. There will be setbacks and moments where we feel compelled to revert to the familiar, but that is the worst thing we can do. The grit, hard work, and determination needed to reset will teach us more about who we are and what we can do. When we put in the work, we will emerge new and better. However, we must remember this is not a zero-sum game. There will be many times throughout our lives where we are forced to reset because growth occurs over time. It's not finite.

So what is the come up? It's the way you level up in relation to you. It's how we beat the odds and the way we move beyond circumstances to be more for ourselves (and indirectly, others). It's selfless contentment grounded in becoming our best self on our terms. It's looking in the mirror and being happy that we could have more, but we are appreciative that we don't have less. It is knowing that we put in the work, and because we did, all will be well.

The come up is in the real work that allows us to see beyond sex, beyond scams, and beyond survival to create our best life. Beyond *sex* means we don't have to use our femininity (or masculinity) to level up. We allow people to see us for what we know and not our physical appearance. Beyond *scams* means we are not hustling in the negative to come up. We've found value in patience and persistence and we use those attributes to move into the next phase of our lives. Beyond *survival* means we will find the fortitude and resilience needed to continue to truly live. We're not living every day trying to figure out how we will get by. Instead, we create a plan and we leverage all our resources to come all the way up.

In the end, you will define your come up. I just want you to know all you desire can be acquired if you believe in yourself and stay the course. Take it from a little girl from Brooklyn, who learned the value of a dream, who saw worth in her elders and who wasn't afraid to step out on her own (with God's grace and mercy) and do the work. She may not have the best of all things but she sleeps comfortably at night and wakes up each morning excited about the promise in each day! You can be your own come up, you don't really have any other choice! Do it in patience, in love and in peace and watch the blessings anchor you...trust me, it is the most rewarding feeling in the world.

Remember...

The come up is in the real work

that allows you to see beyond

sex, beyond scams, and beyond

survival to create your best life.

Acknowledgments

I would be remiss if I did not thank God foremost for all the times He has kept me and bestowed His grace and mercy. It has also been through Him that I have fortunate to be born into a loving family unit. My family has been my greatest source of strength and encouragement. I really don't know where I would be without their love and support. Mommy and Daddy, you are my foundation. You two have sacrificed your lives for your children and your family; know that those sacrifices have not gone unnoticed.

My family: Each of you have poured into me in your own unique way. Anthony, Aleshia, and Arlene, I couldn't have been blessed better siblings—Lesha, never forget you paved the way; I would not have had the opportunities afforded to me had you not developed a stellar academic and personal reputation that set an expectation. To all of my cousins, near and far, know that you are loved. Peaches, Charlene, Jada, Adrienne, Hans, Kendra, and Nakaita, you're more than cousins, you are my sisters and my first friends (despite the occasional quarrel LOL),

I thank you for the love and support especially on this particular journey. Traci, Binta, and Karen you are and have always been my toughest critics, but I've grown so much as a woman under your watchful hands. Traci you have guided me through high school, into my career to this very moment. For every argument, tear, and pause, I thank you and I love you!

Charles and Lee (RIP), you sheltered me from harm's way ... the real talk and the laughs will forever be treasured. I was never too big or too old for loving reprimand. Marcus, I appreciate all the joy you have brought to my sister and our family. All of my uncles have served as second fathers and protectors: Solo (RIP), Trevor, Wayne, Charles (RIP), Derrick, Glen, Joey, Peter, Junior, Carlyle and Alwin—I love you guys. To my aunties who have fed me in more ways than one, know that you are truly appreciated: Creola, Marina, Shery Ann, Cheryl, Vicki, Janice, Allyson, Muriel, and Alliene. And my babies...Tiana, Tamia, Tinayah, Mekhi, Sanai, Cyiana, Jenee, Kayla, Kaliegh, and Buddha (Anthony) ... auntie loves you! Let this project remind you that your wildest dreams can become a reality—and I'll be here to see them through.

Moneca Jackson, outside of my immediate family, you were the first young woman on Putnam I noticed who made a conscious decision to walk boldly into her dreams. You will never know what a profound impact your journey has had on my career as an educator. To my friends Natascha Jackson, Stephanie Tabertus, Sinthia Amaya, Lionel Christian and Paul Taylor, — words will never be enough to fully explain the ways you have shown up for me and breathed life into my dream—this book.

To my mentors and sages: Gloria Carter, Carolyn Archer, Dr. Frank Mickens, Dr. Bernard Gassaway, Ruth Lovelace, Stan Kinard, Evan Murray, Sabrina Parham, Paul Tudor Jones, Timphony Blakeney, Cheryl Lewis, Sheila Shale, Drs. Renee and Lester Young, Donnie Harris, Nebert Jackson, and Terry-Arlene Marshall—your guidance has helped me grow and develop as a woman. Your listening ear and thoughtful reproach have moved me into greater spaces. And to my Shawn

Carter Foundation (Ms. G, Ms. C, Chaka Pilgrim, Paul Taylor, Nyoka Gracey, Kyle Hall, Alonda DuVall, and Dania Diaz—love you all), Adelaide Sanford Institute, Emmanuel Baptist Church (Chosen Women's Ministry), West Indian American Day Carnival Association, Teachers College UELP Cohort 2017, Boys and Girls High School and Medgar Evers College Preparatory School families, our work shows that together we can make a difference. Thank you.

POP, you've helped me weather many storms. I can always count on you and I could not ask for a better friend (thanks Darry). Willow, Genesa Campbell, Tamika Cobb, (love y'all so much Nes and Mikks—we fight but we've been loving on each other for a quarter, thanks for the consistency besties), Margaret McNeil, Isha Moseley (Ro-Mo; my sisters—so much more than friends), Delissa John (my biggest cheerleader), Carmin Wong, Tiffany Smith, Krystal Allen, Russelle Jno-Lewis, Quinn Fields, Karen St. Hilaire, Angela Terry, Nadia Lopez, Amika Henneman, Reshma Ramarack, Sydney Knox, Corina

McCallum, Linda Sanders-Peay, Bino, Joel Cox, Arlis Michaels, Alexica Samms, Tajuana Watson, Kim Barron, Celina Acham, Alwin Jones, Gerdie Renee-Gordon, Alybania DeLaCruz, , Sheila Bonilla, Lucy Trigueno, La'Tikka Cannon, Kilolo Moyo, Rashida Mays, Nessa Williams, Chanel George, Kirrick Wise, Joey Walker, Shane Andrews, Ronnie Johnson, Carl Swygert, Jamal Lovelace, Chris Smith, Calito, Billie, Halston, Dub, C-Man, Mann, Jules, Anyanwu and Tishara Joseph —your friendship continues to move mountains in my life.

My angels in heaven: you comfort and carry me, you go before me and make my ways straight. You have made a way when there was no way. Although I would want nothing more than to have another hug or conversation or to simply see those smiles, I know that you are in heaven celebrating this very moment. Although my heart is heavy and will be until we meet again, I hope I have, in some way, honored you and made you all proud.

The Trini blood flowing through my veins compels me to acknowledge every Soca artist on my iPhone playlist, know that the *Soca Kingdom* kept me going ... the long nights were possible because every *Good Morning* was met with a *Hello*. And, when I was *In the Middle of Something*, Soca somehow helped to center my *State of Mind*, because God alone knows, this project was *Overdue*. Somehow, I managed to be *Brave* even when I had to tell people to Miss Me Wid Dat or *Leave Me Alone* with *No Apology* and I simply accepted all the *Splinters* along the way. But, more importantly, this period in my life is one that has taught me to embrace being a *Loner* because it really is about *D'Journey*. Although I'm *Far From Finished*, I know I can go the *Full Extreme* and drift on *Cloud 9*... so, thank you Soca, this was truly a *Road Trip!*

Finally, I have to thank all of my students for the ways in which you have allowed me to serve you over the years. Through the talks, letters, texts, and even disagreements, I have grown as an educator, a learner, and

124

a woman. You are truly the reason. You give me purpose and hope; most importantly, each of you has helped to shape the work I do every day—some days are tough but knowing that you all are counting on me motivates me to keep showing up. There's a quote I often see on Instagram and Facebook that says, "I want to inspire people. I want someone to look at me and say, 'Because of you I didn't give up'" I hope my life's work will be a testament to that very idea. And it is my hope that this book is my opportunity to touch more young people and impact who they will become as well. Ensuring a better life for you is the reason for every life sacrifice I have made.

So, to every young woman <u>and</u> young man who reads this book, remember, your current circumstances do not define you. Once you learn to be your own come up, you can walk through life knowing you are truly the prize. Always protect your heart, protect your peace, protect your energy, protect your magic, protect yourself and protect each other.

I'm Listening...

Thanks for taking the time to read this book. I'm looking

forward to your feedback.

Feel free to contact me at beyourowncomeup@gmail.com

Bless,

Andrea

About the Author

Currently serving as an Assistant Principal in Brooklyn, New York, Andrea Toussaint has been in the field of education for over 15 years. Her love for her community and commitment to students has made her an indispensable resource. After earning a bachelor's degree from Lincoln University in 2002, she returned to her high school alma mater, Boys and Girls HS, under the leadership of Dr. Frank N. Mickens where she provided students with what she herself received as a young person: caring relationships with teachers, mentoring and a passion for learning.

Andrea is someone who recognizes herself in her students, a teacher who embodies the sister, aunt and friend that many young people need in their lives. Ms. Toussaint strives to learn so she can share with others, and her goal to give back every day has helped to inspire countless young people. She is known as an educator who goes beyond the call of duty for her students and her school.

With master's degrees from New York University, the College of St. Rose, and Columbia University, Andrea is working towards completing her doctoral degree at Teachers College, Columbia University in May of 2020. She currently resides in Brooklyn, New York.

References

1. Shakur, T. (2009). The rose that grew from concrete. New York: MTV Books/Pocket Books. (ref p.20)
2. "promise." Merriam-Webster.com. 2011. https://www.merriam-webster.com (8 May 2011). (ref p.30)
3. The Holy Bible: New International Version. Zondervan, 1984. (ref p.41)
4. Twerski, A. (2016). How do lobsters grow? YouTube. https://www.youtube.com/watch?v=dcUAlpZrwog. (ref p. 50)

Proofread by Dr. Bernard Gassaway

Edited by Carmin Wong @dearbrothermalcolm and Bookbaby.com

Cover Photography, Layout & Design by Stephanie Tabertus @tabertus.jpg

Styled for Cover by Natascha Jackson @prettygirlzfit

Makeup by Marshalle Crockett @marshallecorckett

Hair by Ming @hairby.ming

Production Team: Shantelle Francis, Charlene Joseph and Arlene Toussaint

Manager: Aleshia T. Toussaint   aihselal003@yahoo.com

Executive Assistant: Sinthia Amaya   sincerelytheexecutiveassistant@gmail.com

Public Relations: Lionel A. Christian   lionelchristian@gmail.com

Graphic Designer: Stephanie Tabertus www.tabertus.com

FOLLOW on Instagram @BEYOUROWNCOMEUP or @dre_a_t

EMAIL beyourowncomeup@gmail.com

Made in the USA
Middletown, DE
23 August 2019